IMAGES
of America

SAN DIEGO
POLICE DEPARTMENT

COVER: This image is from the late 1950s. Patrol officers line up as Sgt. James Slack conducts a weapons inspection in the center courtyard patio of police headquarters. (Courtesy of E.W. Kenney historic collection of the San Diego Police Museum.)

IMAGES
of America

SAN DIEGO
POLICE DEPARTMENT

Steve Willard
Foreword by Chief William Lansdowne

ARCADIA

Published by Arcadia Publishing
Charleston SC, Chicago IL, Portsmouth NH, San Francisco CA

Printed in Great Britain

Library of Congress Catalog Card Number: 2005925460

For all general information contact Arcadia Publishing at:
Telephone 843-853-2070
Fax 843-853-0044
E-mail sales@arcadiapublishing.com
For customer service and orders:
Toll-Free 1-888-313-2665

Visit us on the internet at http://www.arcadiapublishing.com

CONTENTS

FOREWORD

San Diego is California's second largest city and it is the seventh largest in the nation. The city boasts a population of nearly 1.3 million residents and geographically covers more than 324 square miles. San Diego is known for its near-idyllic climate, miles of pristine beaches, and a dazzling array of world-class family attractions, including the world-famous San Diego Zoo, the Wild Animal Park, and Sea World San Diego.

The Pacific Ocean coastline supports year-round outdoor recreation such as surfing, boating, sailing, and swimming; and important scientific research is done at the Scripps Institution of Oceanography. San Diego is home to Balboa Park, the largest urban cultural park in the United States, featuring 15 museums, numerous art galleries, beautiful gardens, and the Tony Award–winning Globe Theatre. The city has grown from a once sleepy military town to a bustling urban metropolis that supports National Football League and Major League Baseball sports franchises and multi-million dollar venues.

The history of law enforcement in San Diego evolved through the years to keep pace with the growth of over 100 distinct communities. The office of the San Diego City Marshal operated from 1850 until 1889, when the San Diego Police Department (SDPD) was established. In May of 1939, the SDPD moved into the historic police headquarters at 801 West Market Street. In January 1986, the SDPD moved into 1401 Broadway where the current facility houses a state-of-the-art communications section, a crime laboratory, and offices for the chief of police, criminal intelligence, homicide, sex crimes, robbery, and many other investigative teams and support groups.

Gone are the days of call boxes, which have been replaced by high-level communications technology. Today, officers patrol their community on foot, on bicycles, on horseback, in cars and motorcycles, and by plane and helicopter. The modern police officer carries an array of resources including cellular phones, laptop computers capable of linking major databases and receiving calls for service, along with less-lethal tools like baton launchers and Taser guns.

Throughout several decades of public service, many fine men and women have contributed great insight and guidance into building the San Diego Police Department. Their commitment to public safety and the community they serve has demonstrated that the department truly is "America's Finest." It is with great honor that I dedicate this book to all the members, past and present, of the San Diego Police Department.

—William M. Lansdowne
Chief of Police

Chief William Lansdowne heads the almost 2,600-member San Diego Police Department. A veteran of more than 37 years, Lansdowne began his law enforcement career in San Jose, California, eventually serving as chief both there and in Richmond, California, prior to heading south. He was sworn in as the SDPD chief in August 2003.

ACKNOWLEDGMENTS

I would like start off by thanking the men and women of the San Diego Police Department. They have valiantly served this city for more than a century and even though it would be impossible to fully document more than 100 years of police work, hopefully this book is at least a step in the right direction.

I want to apologize to anyone I forgot to list here, and I hope you realize it's my error and not a lack of appreciation. Without the foresight of individuals such as the late Pliney Castanien and the late Sgt. Edward W. Kenney, who began collecting artifacts and documenting the history of the SDPD from as early as the 1950s, this book would not have been possible. Photojournalist Bob Lampert used his camera from the 1960s to the 1990s to capture much of the SDPD's history. Photographer Sandy Small brought her 35-millimeter camera on a number of ride-a-longs and managed to capture history as it unfolded. Lt. Tom Giaquinto and Sgt. Gary Mitrovich kept history alive throughout the 1980s and 1990s by writing a number of interesting articles on SDPD history. To this day, retired officers such as Capt. Dave Crow, Lts. Chuck Ellison, Jim Caster, and Allen Brown, Sgt. Stan Elmore, and Det. Richard Allen all work to keep retired officers in touch with one another.

Even with all of the goodwill there still needed to be a museum to display it all. Officers John Graham and Matt Weathersby, among others, floated ideas of creating a museum almost 20 years ago, but the timing wasn't right. In 1997, things seemed to align perfectly, and the San Diego Police Historical Association was formed by Officer Doug English, Det. John Minto, Sgt. Gary Mitrovich, and retired officer Gary Dennis. These men also set about to stop the impending demolition of the historic police headquarters at 801 West Market Street. They hired preservationist Vonn Marie May to nominate the building for the prestigious National Register of Historic Places, and in 1998 it became only the 25th police facility in the country to ever become a national landmark.

In 1998, detective Rick Carlson and I joined the board. Together, our organization worked diligently to open a temporary museum downtown at 205 G Street in early 2000. We then partnered with preservationists, civic groups, and elected officials to see the old police headquarters saved once and for all.

Today, the San Diego Police Historical Association is run by a nine-member board of directors who are all dedicated to keep the legacy of America's finest police department alive, and we anticipate more success in the years to come.

INTRODUCTION

In 1769, Friar Junipero Serra established the first mission in California, and on July 17, San Diego was officially founded. Under Serra, law enforcement was simple—unmarried citizens were locked in the barracks at night to prevent temptation.

In 1821, San Diego became part of Mexico, and on January 1, 1836, she was officially named "El Puebla De San Diego De Acala." By 1838, the population had decreased; the town was stripped of its puebla status and designated an outward suburb of Los Angeles. Despite the small population as a frontier town, violence was common. After months of witnessing the lawlessness, Antonio Gonzales and eight men formed a small police force. They kept the peace until 1845, when the U.S. Army took over. The soldiers dealt with crime by shooting troublemakers.

In May 1850, San Diego was incorporated as an American city and Agoston Haraszathy was elected city marshal. He appointed Richard Freeman as his deputy, making him the first African-American lawman in California. That summer, Haraszathy constructed a $5,000 jail, but unfortunately the mud-brick facility melted in the first heavy rain. Another $2,000 was invested, but within hours of being arrested, the first inmate, 25-year-old Roy Bean, escaped by digging through the walls. Decades later, Bean would establish himself in Langford, Texas, as the "Law West of the Pecos."

Agoston Haraszathy left town in December 1851 to serve in the state assembly, and later as the first assayer of the San Francisco Mint. He also founded the California wine industry.

As a result of the jail debacle, in 1852 San Diego filed bankruptcy and the state repealed its charter. With city services suspended, the quality of life suffered. Crime quickly returned as decent citizens hid in their homes while armed gangs walked the streets.

Law and order began a comeback in 1861, when an iron cage was used as a jail in back of city hall. By 1862, the finances improved enough for a marshal to be appointed.

For the next 17 years, the marshal's top priority would be tax collection and building roads. To keep the peace, Mexicans and Native Americans were barred from coming within a half mile of the city. By 1879, the job of marshal was not a paid position, and there were no applicants, so the city abolished the position.

By 1885, the city was one of the most violent places in North America. To control it, the city marshal was reestablished with 25 men. Because of politics, they were horribly ineffective.

By 1889, the population was more than 40,000, and an entire part of downtown hosted opium dens and brothels 24 hours a day. People carried guns openly, and marshals were nowhere to be found. The new, bawdy district was named the Stingaree, and it gave San Diego all the characteristics of an out-of-control circus.

The answer to the problem would come in the form of a new city charter with a municipal police department whose officers' foremost job was fighting crime. They took to the streets on

June 1, 1889, armed with new powers and a single purpose. By the end of 1889 they had regained control, but working conditions had taken a toll. Of the 12 officers hired in May, 5 had resigned. By the end of 1917, the city had filled the office of chief 13 times. The reason was a continuing struggle with city hall over who would control the SDPD.

The Great Depression hit the police department hard. Faced with a budget so tight that 20 percent of the department faced layoffs, the officers still found ways to get new uniforms, equipment, and cars. They also voted themselves a pay cut so no one would be let go. The 1930s saw the introduction of a new city charter that expressly forbade council influence over the SDPD. It was a deathblow to political influence and nepotism.

World War II was hard for the SDPD. In addition to a third of its officers being drafted, the population of the city doubled. Officers worked 12 to 18 hours a day, seven days a week. Housing shortages were so severe many people slept in hotel beds in shifts. Soldiers flooded downtown bars 24 hours a day, and there were fights galore.

Towards the end of World War II, the SDPD opened a police school for new officers. In 1947, rules were instituted outlawing drinking, picking up dates, and gratuities. It was the birth of the modern, professional police officer.

The 1950s saw the issue of low staffing brought to the forefront. Instead of hiring additional officers, the department instead adopted a "one officer per car" policy. The 1960s saw unrest across the country. San Diego was also forced to deal with riots and antiwar demonstrations.

On September 25, 1978, the worst airline disaster in the city's history occurred when a Boeing 727 crashed in a neighborhood, killing 144 people. Police recruits were brought in for search and rescue. For some, the carnage was so much that it marked their last day in law enforcement. As the 1970s ended, the SDPD was losing officers at rates never before seen. In addition to leaving for better jobs, they were also being murdered.

By the mid-1980s, San Diego was not only the deadliest city for police officers to work in per capita, it was also its lowest staffed per population ratio. The 1990s saw an aggressive push to train officers in new and innovative safety tactics, effectively lowering the officer mortality rate to the lowest in the country for a large city.

As the 20th century drew to a close, SDPD personnel had handled mass murder, serial killers, two Super Bowls, a Republican National Convention, riots, shootouts, and two world wars. They are still understaffed despite having more than 2,100 officers, 600 support personnel, and over 1,000 volunteers. The ethnic makeup and gender diversity of the department more accurately reflects the community as it evolved into a new millennium.

One
CITY MARSHALS

The first decades of city law enforcement were haphazard at best. Between 1850 and 1889, the office of the city marshal was disbanded and reestablished a number of times. The city did not mandate their priorities as law enforcement, and appointments to the marshal's office were based on nepotism. Not surprisingly, the men were largely ineffective in dealing with crime. By 1889, crime was so out of control that the only way to regain it was to abolish the marshals and replace them with police officers. By the end of the year, civility began to make a comeback on San Diego's streets.

Although they wore San Diego Police badges, these deputy city marshals were more tax collectors than lawmen. In an effort to save money, the City also tasked them with issuing gambling permits, running the chain gang, and even building roads and hospitals. (Courtesy of E.W. Kenney historic collection of the San Diego Police Museum.)

San Diego's first city marshal, Agoston Haraszathy, was a Hungarian count and one of the wealthiest immigrants to the United States in the 1800s. Appointed marshal in 1850, Haraszathy chose former slave Richard Freeman to be his deputy, making him the first African-American lawman in California. After leaving San Diego, Haraszathy founded the California wine industry. His creation, Zinfandel, is still being produced in Sonoma County. He died in Nicaragua in 1869 when he was eaten by crocodiles. (Courtesy of E.W. Kenney historic collection of the San Diego Police Museum.)

These 1886 deputy city marshals were not effective lawmen. They were controlled by the city fathers, the hours were long (12 hours a day, seven days a week), and the monthly pay was $75. Uniforms alone cost $42.50. (Courtesy of E.W. Kenney historic collection of the San Diego Police Museum.)

Deputy city marshal Jesse B. Cook began his law enforcement career in San Diego in 1885, but it was in San Francisco that he made a name for himself. Cook joined the SFPD in 1888 and was on hand to witness the great earthquake of 1906. He became chief of police shortly thereafter and served until the 1930s, when he became an SFPD police commissioner. (Courtesy of E.W. Kenney historic collection of the San Diego Police Museum.)

Joe Coyne served as sheriff prior to his tenure as the last city marshal and first SDPD chief. Coyne came to the job not needing the money, having amassed a small fortune in a mining operation in Julian. With a new city charter in place, Coyne was allowed to make law enforcement his top priority. Within months, his officers did what he couldn't do as marshal— get a grip on crime. Coyne would be proud to know that 100 years after he served, his great-granddaughter, Laura McGowan, also became an SDPD officer. (Courtesy of E.W. Kenney historic collection of the San Diego Police Museum.)

Assistant city marshal Leroy P. Barton was Marshal Joe Coyne's right hand man. When the San Diego Police Department was formed in 1889, he became the first assistant chief of police. (Courtesy of E.W. Kenney historic collection of the San Diego Police Museum.)

Sixty-three-year-old deputy city marshal Thomas "Uncle Tom" O'Rourke wore badge no. 1 and was commonly referred to as San Diego's first policeman. For the two years he served, he was one of the busiest men on the force and led the agency in arrests, most of them for an ambiguous section known as Ordinance 19. Thomas O'Rourke died in the line of duty in September 1888. (Courtesy of E.W. Kenney historic collection of the San Diego Police Museum.)

Frank Northern was a veteran of the Civil War and served as a deputy city marshal from 1887 until the office was disbanded in 1889. He joined the SDPD months later and went on to serve a 22-year career when, in 1911, he became the first officer to ever retire from the department. He died in 1941 at the age of 96. (Courtesy of E.W. Kenney historic collection of the San Diego Police Museum.)

Two
PEOPLE OF THE SDPD

Since 1889, more than 10,000 men and women have served as SDPD officers. Some have been hugely successful while others were scantly noticed. The men and women of the SDPD have, by and large, been innovators in their field. San Diego employed a black law enforcement officer 13 years before the Emancipation Proclamation, and employed female officers years before their civilian counterparts were given the right to vote. In more modern times, San Diego was a pioneering agency of the Neighborhood Watch program and community-oriented policing. These are just a few of the many who have helped create America's finest police department.

Most of the men in this 1897 photo with Chief James Russell (center) are new or rehires. Because of a poor economy two years prior, the force had dwindled down to just six men. (Courtesy of E.W. Kenney historic collection of the San Diego Police Museum.)

James Russell served as a city constable, deputy city marshal, acting city marshal, and finally chief of police. As chief, Russell did good job and because he was able to secure better working conditions and raises for his officers, he was very popular. Yet when he backed the wrong person for mayor and he lost, his days in office were numbered. (Courtesy of E.W. Kenney historic collection of the San Diego Police Museum.)

Edward "Ned" Bushyhead was a founder of the *San Diego Union* newspaper and served both as sheriff and a police commissioner prior to his becoming SDPDs chief in 1899. A Cherokee, Bushyhead was a lawman at a time when it was illegal for a Native Americans to testify in court against a white man. (Courtesy of E.W. Kenney historic collection of the San Diego Police Museum.)

Even though the SDPD was very progressive in hiring a black officer in 1909, not everyone was so open-minded. This outwardly racist cartoon of Officer Frank McCarter appeared in the *San Diego Sun* shortly after the hiring was announced. McCarter went on to serve the SDPD until 1915. (Courtesy of E.W. Kenney historic collection of the San Diego Police Museum.)

Bartholomew Moriority served San Diego first as a deputy city marshal before becoming 1 of the 12 original officers hired by SDPD in 1889. During his career, he headed the detective bureau and became the department's first captain before his 1915 retirement. (Courtesy of E.W. Kenney historic collection of the San Diego Police Museum.)

There were only six other men on the SDPD when George Pringle pinned on his seven-point star on December 31, 1894. Pringle later described his first days as a raw-knuckle job where a cop relied on his wits and strength for survival. The son of SDPD's third chief, Pringle served more than 41 years as an SDPD officer. His tenure set a record for sworn officers. At his retirement, the 71-year-old sergeant said he just wanted to go out and have some fun. He died in 1943. (Courtesy of E.W. Kenney historic collection of the San Diego Police Museum.)

Chief Keno Wilson (right) meets San Diego's first police chief, 101-year-old Antonio Gonzales, in 1911. The old chief served from 1838 to 1845, at a time when San Diego was under Mexican rule. He came back to town after he was robbed in Mexico. Recognizing the historical significance, Wilson found a photographer to take their picture in front of police headquarters. (Courtesy of Francis Jansen.)

Ida Griffin (pictured) is often credited as SDPD's first female employee and its first policewoman. Both titles are inaccurate. The first female employee of the SDPD was Matron Rose Longacre, who was hired in January of 1912, beating Griffin to the job by three months. The SDPD's first policewoman was Lucille Jeardue, hired in July 1917. (Courtesy of E.W. Kenney historic collection of the San Diego Police Museum.)

Not many San Diegans are aware that East San Diego was once an independent city. Its western border was Boundary Street. East San Diego's chief law enforcement officer, Frank Hyatt, also served as city tax collector. (Courtesy of San Diego Police Museum.)

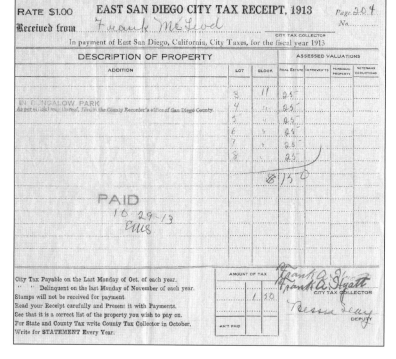

Nat McHorney Jr. served as the last chief of the East San Diego Police Department and saw the sun set on what had once been called "The Golden Rule City." On January 1, 1924, the entire ESDPD was absorbed into the SDPD and East San Diego ceased to exist. McHorney and his five officers worked out of a station located at 4254 University Avenue. The address was a part of a much larger building that housed city hall and the fire department. (Courtesy of Rea McHorney.)

Spade Burns was a wiry, cigar-chomping chief lifeguard for the SDPD from 1923 until the unit was placed under the park and recreation department in 1947. Burns headed a crew of lifeguards patrolling the beaches and the men saved hundreds of San Diegans from death in the water. It was said that Burns was so angry that he quit the lifeguard service after Chief Elmer Jansen transferred the men out of the SDPD. (Courtesy of E.W. Kenney historic collection of the San Diego Police Museum.)

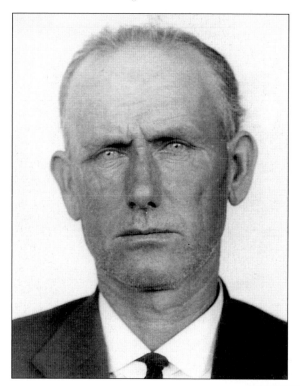

Charles Harris was a 51-year-old detective when he was shot and killed in the line of duty on April 3, 1927, during a stakeout in Balboa Park. His policewoman partner, Officer Rena Wright, led an unsuccessful search of the park to locate the killer. The case has never been solved. (Courtesy of E.W. Kenney historic collection of the San Diego Police Museum.)

Officer John Cloud was SDPD's first African-American sergeant and the first black officer to serve a 20-year career. Cloud was hired in 1918 as a civilian chauffer, but within months he became a sworn officer. When he retired, he was one of the department's most respected men. (Courtesy of E.W. Kenney historic collection of the San Diego Police Museum.)

Range master Rodney Pease uses his large diamond ring as a mirror to shoot a bull's eye over his shoulder. In addition to his trick shooting, Pease was a world champion shot in the competitive circuit. During his 20-year career, Pease built a pistol range and taught every officer how to shoot their weapons in combat scenarios. Rodney Pease retired from the SDPD in 1950 and enjoyed a long retirement before his death in 2001 at the age of 99. (Courtesy of E.W. Kenney historic collection of the San Diego Police Museum.)

Harry Raymond (dark suit, white hat) was an LAPD detective when he became SDPD's chief in June 1933. He was fired in September when he angered the city manager by enforcing vice laws downtown. After Raymond left San Diego he went back to Los Angeles, where he conducted an investigation on corruption in city hall. As he was about to deliver his evidence, his car exploded with him in it. Raymond survived, and his evidence led to Mayor Frank Shaw being recalled, LAPD chief James E. Davis resigning, and LAPD brass going to prison. (Courtesy of E.W. Kenney historic collection of the San Diego Police Museum.)

Chief George Sears and J. Edgar Hoover managed a get-together during the legendary FBI director's visit to the 1935 exposition. The 1930s were a tumultuous time for the SDPD, and between 1930 and 1940, the office of chief was filled 11 times. Even more amazing was that Sears was chief for 5 of those 10 years. (Courtesy of E.W. Kenney historic collection of the San Diego Police Museum.)

While many police officers are ambitious, one man, Adam Elmer Jansen, had his sights set on becoming chief from the first day he pinned on a badge. He made it 15 years later and within hours began transferring people and issuing official orders. Jansen served as chief from 1947 to 1962, when he left to become San Diego county sheriff. His 15 years as an SDPD chief will likely never be matched. (Courtesy of E.W. Kenney historic collection of the San Diego Police Museum.)

Det. William "Bert" Ritchey was the SDPD's first African-American homicide detective and deserves much of the credit for forming the department's crime laboratory. Ritchey had most of the lab's equipment donated by a wealthy friend and he spent a lot of his own time learning forensics. Ritchey was considered a master of photography and fingerprints, and his skills solved many crimes. He served the SDPD from 1932 until 1964, when he left to become one of San Diego's most successful attorneys. (Courtesy of E.W. Kenney historic collection of the San Diego Police Museum.)

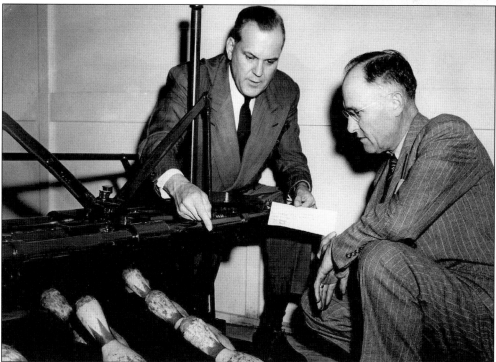

Chief Clifford Peterson uses the police bowling alley as a prop to present the check that paid for its installation. Peterson came to the SDPD in 1940 having served as a police lieutenant in Long Beach. He guided the department through the lean times of World War II, but when it ended, he began to look for new challenges. He left in November 1947 to become commissioner of the California Highway Patrol. (Courtesy of E.W. Kenney historic collection of the San Diego Police Museum.)

Dispatcher Billie Bond (Crow) relays a call for service to patrol units in the field. Billie served the SDPD from 1958 to 1993. She only remained retired for a short time before coming back as a part-time employee and serving another 10 years. (Courtesy of E.W. Kenney historic collection of the San Diego Police Museum.)

William B. Kolender took office as acting chief in September 1975, and in February 1976, he was officially appointed. At age 40, Kolender was one of the youngest big-city chiefs in the country. He served 13 years as chief and during his reign he made the department more diverse and community-oriented. He left the SDPD in 1988, but returned to law enforcement first as the head of the California Youth Authority and then San Diego County Sheriff. (Courtesy of E.W. Kenney historic collection of the San Diego Police Museum.)

Richard Bennett first joined the SDPD as a police cadet on October 2, 1961. When he ended his career as a lieutenant on March 31, 2002, he became the longest tenured full-time employee in the history of the SDPD. (Courtesy of E.W. Kenney historic collection of the San Diego Police Museum.)

Connie Borchers (Van Putten) was first hired as a policewoman in 1965, knowing the job would not allow her uniformed patrol duties. That didn't stop her from working hard, as court cases in other cities were making an impact on attitudes toward the integration of women into fieldwork in the SDPD. In 1976, she was promoted to sergeant, becoming the first woman in SDPD history to hold a supervisory position. (Courtesy of E.W. Kenney historic collection of the San Diego Police Museum.)

Alicia Daly-Lampert (in early 1970s formal uniform) was SDPD's first uniformed female patrol officer. On April 17, 1973, she took to the streets, and within days others followed. In 1974, the titles of policewoman and patrolman were officially abolished and replaced with the generic title of police officer. (Courtesy of E.W. Kenney historic collection of the San Diego Police Museum.)

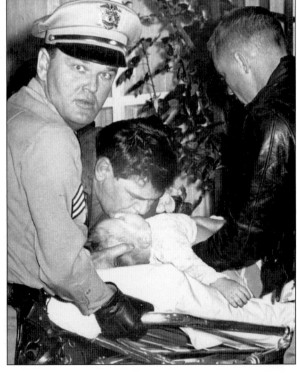

Sgt. Edward W. Kenney reacts with surprise to the photographer during a call of a non-breathing baby. During his tenure with the SDPD, Kenney collected thousands of artifacts and photographs of the department. He also interviewed retired officers, some who had served as far back as 1908. When Kenney passed away in 1998, his widow began transferring his collection to the San Diego Police Historical Association. The collection is so large that it is the backbone of the museum. (Courtesy of E.W. Kenney historic collection of the San Diego Police Museum.)

Sgt. Rulette Armstead wasn't the first African-American female to serve the SDPD. That honor went to Helga Johnson, who was hired a year before. Armstead was the department's first female African-American sergeant and is now, as assistant chief of police, of equal standing with Cheryl Meyers as SDPD's highest-ranking active-duty female officer. (Courtesy of E.W. Kenney historic collection of the San Diego Police Museum.)

The SDPD doesn't have an age limit for recruits, and there are a number of men and women who serve as a second career. Mel Allen is one example. A former sergeant major who served a 24-year career in the Marine Corps, Allen was a decorated Vietnam War veteran when he was sworn in with the SDPD in 1988. (Courtesy of E.W. Kenney historic collection of the San Diego Police Museum.)

The Collins family has a tradition of service within the SDPD. Patriarch Cliff Collins served from 1954 to 1980. He was still active when his son Jim joined in 1972. Jim and former wife Linda were serving as SDPD officers when their son Ted was born. He was the first child born to two SDPD officers. Ted joined the SDPD in 2002, and has worked with his dad. (Courtesy of San Diego Police Museum archives and Jim Collins.)

Three
PLACES OF THE SDPD

There are a number of places with historic relevance to the SDPD. Historically speaking, one of the most important locations to the SDPD is the old police headquarters at 801 West Market Street. The 98,000-square-foot facility opened on the 50th anniversary of the SDPD on May 9, 1939, and served almost 50 years before overcrowding lead to its abandonment. Today, the building enjoys the prestige of being only the 25th police facility in the country to ever be recognized as a national landmark. In 2004, the building's owner, the San Diego Unified Port District, concluded an eight-year fight to save the building when they agreed to restore it as a commercial operation.

The 1850 cobblestone jail will be remembered more for how it bankrupted the city than how it served the public. Despite $7,000 being put into its 1850 construction and remodeling, the jail only held one inmate, 25-year-old Roy Bean, who dug his way through the walls and escaped. Later in his life, Bean showed up in Texas, where he was known as "The Hanging Judge." (Courtesy of E.W. Kenney historic collection of the San Diego Police Museum.)

The first SDPD station was actually a shared facility with the fire department in an area that is now Horton Plaza. Around 1900, the SDPD moved into city hall, located at Fifth and G Streets. The station was on the ground floor and the jail was in the basement. Today, the old city hall houses a restaurant and offices. (Courtesy of E.W. Kenney historic collection of the San Diego Police Museum.)

This is an image of Sgt. George Churchman and his men outside the University Avenue substation in 1925. At the time this photo was taken the area was sparsely populated and on the fringes of the city limits. Today, it is one of San Diego's most densely populated communities. (Courtesy of E.W. Kenney historic collection of the San Diego Police Museum.)

When the East San Diego Police Department folded, its headquarters became Substation No. 3. The officers shared the building with an emergency hospital staffed by a police surgeon as well as the fire department. Lt. James Patrick headed the station prior to his 1927 promotion to chief. (Courtesy of E.W. Kenney historic collection of the San Diego Police Museum.)

For those who like the sun and surf, this 1930s photograph of the Ocean Beach substation makes it look like one of the best locations in town to work. Closed for police use in the 1950s when it was decided to have all officers' work out of police headquarters, the building was taken over as a lifeguard station. (Courtesy of E.W. Kenney historic collection of the San Diego Police Museum.)

Not surprisingly, a small bail bond agency sat next to the police station and jail located at 726 Second Street. The buildings, designed by Mayor Edwin Capps, opened in 1911. By the time this 1930s photograph was taken, the buildings were crowded, rat-infested, and falling apart. (Courtesy of E.W. Kenney historic collection of the San Diego Police Museum.)

The alley between the Second Street station and the jail served as parking for the police ambulances. Note the sign above the cars that reads "Emergency Hospital." Ambulances brought injured parties back to the station where they were stabilized by the police surgeon. Those needing long-term care were transferred to local hospitals. (Courtesy of E.W. Kenney historic collection of the San Diego Police Museum.)

Prior to World War II, the city had a tradition of using jail inmates for labor. This 1938 photo is of the city prison camp at Lake Morena, 60 miles east of downtown. Inmates were used to grow food, work on machinery, and serve as a labor pool for other civic projects. (Courtesy of E.W. Kenney historic collection of the San Diego Police Museum.)

Prior to the pistol range being constructed at Home Avenue and Highway 94 in 1935, officers didn't have a place to train with their weapons. Land used for the range was donated to the city and the rocks used in its construction were gathered from a riverbed across the street. The wood was obtained from the 1935 exposition in trade for shooting lessons. Range master Rodney Pease oversaw the construction by jail trustees and he lived at the range until his 1950 retirement. (Courtesy of E.W. Kenney historic collection of the San Diego Police Museum.)

Because of the distance to downtown, the beach community of La Jolla has always had its own substation. This joint fire and police station was used in the 1930s and is today a YMCA. Unlike enclaves such as East San Diego and San Ysidro, La Jolla has never been an independent city. Nonetheless, many residents still question why the SDPD shows up to calls they thought they made to the La Jolla Police Department. (Courtesy of E.W. Kenney historic collection of the San Diego Police Museum.)

This 1940 photo of the old police headquarters gives a stark example of just how unique the iconic building was. Note the large lawn on the front as well as the blend of divergent architecture throughout the facility. (Courtesy of San Diego Police Museum archives.)

The blue neon sign over the arch is long gone, but the most recognizable part of the old police headquarters is its 68-foot tower. While the tower was built largely just for looks, during World War II it served as an observation post for enemy aircraft. When the war ended, the police radio room was located in it for a short period of time. (Courtesy of E.W. Kenney historic collection of the San Diego Police Museum.)

The courtyard of the old police headquarters looked more like a park than a police facility. At the time it opened, the courtyard was landscaped with grass, flowers, trees, fountains, and even terra-cotta tile benches. By the 1960s, it had all been removed for additional parking. (Courtesy of E.W. Kenney historic collection of the San Diego Police Museum.)

As America waged a highly publicized war against public enemies in the 1930s, the two-tiered "Alcatraz" jail design became very popular. Convicts looking through bars as guards walked by on the catwalks became everyone's image of what a jail should look like. (Courtesy of E.W. Kenney historic collection of the San Diego Police Museum.)

The southern division had been open for less than a year when this 1958 photograph was taken. The division encompasses several communities that were once part of the independent city of San Ysidro. Prior to its 1957 annexation, the community was patrolled by the San Diego County Sheriffs Department. (Courtesy of E.W. Kenney historic collection of the San Diego Police Museum.)

When 801 West Market closed in 1987, it was replaced with a $43-million, seven-story headquarters at 1401 Broadway. Despite all of the foresight that went into the building, it quickly fell victim to the very thing that closed the old police headquarters—overcrowding. Within a few years of opening, the department found itself planning to relocate the central patrol division and several detective units to create more room in the headquarters. (Courtesy of Sandra Small collection of the San Diego Police Museum.)

40

Four

THE SCHOOL
SAFETY PATROL

Chief George Sears started the school safety patrol in 1935 after a number of children were fatally injured crossing the street. Chief Sears thought if he could partner officers with responsible children to operate the program, not only would it give the school children a vested interest in the program, it would also save the city money—something that was very important during the Great Depression. More than 20 years after it was started, the school safety patrol program was far more successful than Sears could have ever imagined. An audit into its effectiveness revealed only a handful of children injured in school crossings, none seriously.

Members of the school safety patrol and school children managed to get to the scene even before the police in this 1937 pedestrian-versus-streetcar accident. The accident occurred at 3500 University Avenue, and while the streetcars are long gone, the Wilson Block building still stands. (Courtesy of E.W. Kenney historic collection of the San Diego Police Museum.)

Even the smallest youngsters were involved in the school safety patrol. The uniforms the boys are wearing, white pants and red sweaters, remained consistent until they were abolished in the late 1970s. Badges were added to the uniforms in the 1940s and today are valuable collectors items. (Courtesy of E.W. Kenney historic collection of the San Diego Police Museum.)

Members of the school safety patrol had their own float in this 1938 parade. The banner on the back speaks for itself as to how successful the program has been in just the three years since its founding. (Courtesy of E.W. Kenney historic collection of the San Diego Police Museum.)

Despite the Great Depression not leaving anyone with an abundance of disposable income, officers all chipped in to throw the kids a picnic three days before Christmas in 1938. The officers wanted to show the children they appreciated their hard work and dedication. (Courtesy of E.W. Kenney historic collection of the San Diego Police Museum.)

A school safety patrol boy uses a large stick to keep children on the sidewalk until it is safe to pass. (Courtesy of E.W. Kenney historic collection of the San Diego Police Museum.)

Chief O.J. Roed and three members of the school safety patrol pay a visit in March 1968 to Sea World, where they got to meet one of the park's California sea lions. The boys were being rewarded for being the hardest workers in the patrol that year. (Courtesy of E.W. Kenney historic collection of the San Diego Police Museum.)

It's hard to tell who is having more fun, Sgt. Oscar Johnson or the safety patrol kids. This 1970s photograph showed that the school safety patrol was also an excellent community outreach program for children to interact with police officers. (Courtesy of Bob Lampert.)

Five

DOING THE JOB

Law enforcement is a labor-intensive occupation, so the success of any police department depends upon the support of the community they serve and the quality of the people doing the job. The San Diego Police Department has been very fortunate to not only have a high-percentage approval rating from the general public, they have also employed a number of excellent individuals to serve the community. Perhaps it is why, despite being one of the lowest-staffed police departments in the country, compared to the population it serves, the SDPD still manages to keep crime exceptionally low.

When the International Workers of the World (IWW) came to San Diego in 1912, they were bent on creating anarchy. With the jails full of demonstrators and more on the way, they thought they would be immune from arrest—they were wrong. Instead of being arrested, the men were marched 20 miles out of town, where they were severely beaten and put on trains for Los Angeles with a stern warning not to come back. (Courtesy of E.W. Kenney historic collection of the San Diego Police Museum.)

Police officers use water cannons to disperse IWW protestors in this 1913 photograph. The tactic worked well to disperse the troublemakers, but it was a public relations disaster as the newspapers blasted the department for using excessive force. (Courtesy of E.W. Kenney historic collection of the San Diego Police Museum.)

Much to the surprise of many, the very first SDPD officers walked instead of riding horses. It was not until 1891 that officers were allowed to use a horse as part of their duties. This photo is of Officer Richard Chadwick on patrol around 1911. (Courtesy of E.W. Kenney historic collection of the San Diego Police Museum.)

The first automobiles appeared in San Diego in the very early 1900s and the city recorded its first fatal traffic accident in 1905. Because railroad-crossing signals weren't brought into the city until the 1920s, someone had to stand on the tracks to make sure the train had a clear, safe passage through town. (Courtesy of E.W. Kenney historic collection of the San Diego Police Museum.)

Mounted officers of the SDPD lead a civic parade west down Broadway Street in front of Horton Plaza. The tradition of police participating in parades continues even to this day with the department having a presence in almost every major one throughout the city. (Courtesy of E.W. Kenney historic collection of the San Diego Police Museum.)

Keno Wilson was ahead of his time in many areas, including the establishment of an identification bureau as a central repository of fingerprints, arrest records, mug shots, and crime reports. William Gabrielson (with head down) was tasked with putting it all together. Gabrielson later left the SDPD to become the chief of the Honolulu Police Department. Today, the identification bureau is known as the records division. (Courtesy of E.W. Kenney historic collection of the San Diego Police Museum.)

Officers Walter Holcomb (left) and James Patrick watch as Officer Pat Oviatt answers calls for service in front of the Gamewell communications system. The levers on the system were attached to lights around the city that would signal an officer to call into the station. For an emergency that couldn't wait for an officer to respond to the light, Oviatt would shout out the window to a squad of motorcycle officers sitting at the curb outside headquarters. One of the men would speed to the scene. (Courtesy of E.W. Kenney historic collection of the San Diego Police Museum.)

The 1915 Pan-American Exposition not only put San Diego on the map, it also made Balboa Park a destination and proved that the SDPD was capable of handling large outside events. The exposition wound up being so successful that the city hosted another one 20 years later. Both events were huge economic shots in the arm for San Diego. (Courtesy of E.W. Kenney historic collection of the San Diego Police Museum.)

In addition to increased patrols around the city during the 1915 exposition, a number of officers were hired to work inside the fair itself. In keeping with the exposition's theme, the officers wore special uniforms historically representative of the Spanish colonial era. (Courtesy of E.W. Kenney historic collection of the San Diego Police Museum.)

Almost the entire department turned out to pay their respects to motorcycle officer Joseph S. Lee, killed on March 19, 1921, while chasing a speeder. Officer Lee was passing through the intersection of India and Cedar Street when a gas truck hit him. He was thrown more than 100 feet and died instantly. (Courtesy of E.W. Kenney historic collection of the San Diego Police Museum.)

In the days before sophisticated rescue equipment, officers had to make due with whatever was available. In this 1920s photo, officers and the fire department work together after a car plunged off a cliff. (Courtesy of San Diego Police Museum.)

Det. Lt. George Sears (right) of the Dry Squad poses with a detective in front of the Second Street jail after a 1923 liquor raid. Even though there was some illegal alcohol activity in the city during Prohibition as a border town, San Diego did not have the same problems that existed in many cities across the country. Those wanting a drink simply went south into Mexico where alcohol was not only plentiful and legal, it was also cheap. (Courtesy of E.W. Kenney historic collection of the San Diego Police Museum.)

Motorcycle officers provide an escort for Charles Lindbergh after the famed international pilot toured San Diego following his historic trans-Atlantic flight of May 20, 1927. Not many people are aware that Lindbergh began the first leg of his historic journey in San Diego, or that the *Spirit of St. Louis* was also built here. (Courtesy of E.W. Kenney historic collection of the San Diego Police Museum.)

An officer stops to chat with a boy about safe driving, as the youngster makes his way down the street in a community parade. The pedal car was advertising for the North Park Garage and Gas Station. As one might imagine, the boy didn't get a ticket. The photo was a gag. (Courtesy of E.W. Kenny historic collection of the San Diego Police Museum.)

NOTICE AND PROMISE TO APPEAR FOR TRIAL
FOR VIOLATION OF CALIFORNIA VEHICLE ACT   N⁰ 4767

Driver... *Col Charles Lindbergh*

Address...

Owner... *Same*

Address...

Make of Car... *Spirit of St Louis* Op.) *none*
                                              No.
License No. *No plates* Chauf.) *none*

Location... *Stadium + Flying field* Time... *2.0 pm*

X	Sec.	(Charge indicated by X)	X	Sec.	(Charge indicated by X)
X	51	No Registration Certificate	X	96	Open Cut-out
X	51	No Operator's License	X	121	Reckless Driving
X	51	No Chauffeur's License			
X	125	Cutting In	X	113b	App. Speed *150*
	125c	Passing on Intersection			
X	100	Headlights Out	X	113c	Permissable Speed *20*
X	101	Glaring Headlights	X	130a	No Arm Signal
X	106	No Tail Light			
X	136	Stopping on Highway			

YOU ARE HEREBY NOTIFIED to appear before
C. Chambers City Justice of the Peace, at his office in San Diego, 728 Second St., County of San Diego, State of California, on the *3* day of *February* 192*9*, at the hour of *2* a. m., then and there to answer to a charge of violating the California Vehicle Act of the State of California, the specific charge being indicated above. *A Comstock McC. Neely*
                                              Arresting Officer
I do hereby promise to appear at the time and place and before the Court named in the above notice of arrest, then and there to answer a complaint which may be preferred against me, based on the above notice of arrest.

Dated this *21* day of *September* 192*7*

N. B.—A violation of this promise is a misdemeanor.

Cars weren't the only thing hot-rodding through town as this September 21, 1927 citation to Charles Lindbergh illustrates. The citation is for 150 mph in a 20 mph zone. Lindbergh was also cited for every violation the ticket had printed on it. Of course it was a joke, as his court date was February 31, 1929. (Courtesy of San Diego Police Museum archives.)

Motorcycle officer Tom Remington stands by while a tow-truck driver figures out how to pull a car out of the hole its owner managed to drive into. Prior to World War II, the average San Diegan was far more likely to be killed in a traffic accident than to be murdered. As a result, in 1911 the SDPD began assigning officers to motorcycles with the duties of traffic enforcement. (Courtesy of San Diego Police Museum.)

A May 1933 rally of 300 communists in New Town Park turned violent when protestors began to riot after being told they couldn't display banners without a permit. It took several hours to quell the mayhem and a number of people were injured, including two police officers. (Courtesy of E.W. Kenney historic collection of the San Diego Police Museum.)

The San Diego County Fair in Del Mar is an annual event and the SDPD has a long history of participation. This 1930s exhibit is one of the more elaborate and was done in partnership with the Automobile Club of Southern California. (Courtesy of E.W. Kenney historic collection of the San Diego Police Museum.)

Dispatcher Tommy Thompson takes a break from sending out calls to chat with identification bureau superintendent Walter Macy in this 1935 photograph, taken in what is now known as the Fire Alarm Building at Marston Point. The SDPD first began using radios in December 1932, but they were only one-way and only five cars had them. Thompson and Hebert Holcomb were the SDPDs first dispatchers and worked from 6 a.m. until 2 p.m. For four hours, there was no radio service. By the late 1930s, dispatchers worked 24 hours a day, seven days a week. (Courtesy of E.W. Kenney historic collection of the San Diego Police Museum.)

An officer at the 1935 exposition pauses for a closer look at two cars of the Elks Magazine Goodwill Tour. The cars were just two of many to visit the expo held in Balboa Park that year. (Courtesy of E.W. Kenney historic collection of the San Diego Police Museum.)

Old-time gas station enthusiasts will appreciate this 1937 photograph where officers conduct a DUI checkpoint on Pacific Highway. The SDPD was one of the first police departments in California to use roadblocks as a way to combat drunk drivers. (Courtesy of E.W. Kenney historic collection of the San Diego Police Museum.)

The first SDPD car radios looked more like home telephone receivers than modern police radios. In this 1940 photo, Officer William Warner's car was one of the few patrol vehicles equipped with a two-way radio. It wasn't until after World War II that the equipment became standard in all SDPD cars. (Courtesy of E.W. Kenney historic collection of the San Diego Police Museum.)

Chief George Sears (center) and the SDPD hosted the 1938 International Pistol Competition at the police range. Among those attending were the right- and left-handed pistol champion of the world, LAPD Chief James Edgar Davis (to Sears's right). Months later, Davis was forced to resign as chief when former SDPD chief Harry Raymond survived a car bombing planted by the LAPD and went on to prove he and Los Angeles mayor Frank Shaw were involved in corruption. (Courtesy of E.W. Kenney historic collection of the San Diego Police Museum.)

Officer Robert Karrow and Sgt. Hugh Rochefort practice firing their weapons in the pistol range at police headquarters in this 1939 photograph. Note how narrow the indoor range is and the lack of ear protection. (Courtesy of E.W. Kenney historic collection of the San Diego Police Museum.)

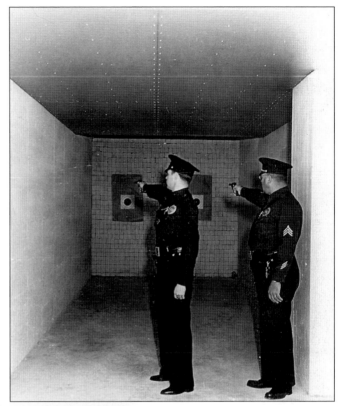

A patrolman, traffic officer, and even the police ambulance driver arrive on the scene of a car over a bridge only to find they are too late. When this early 1940s photo was taken, cars were not equipped with standard seatbelts and airbags, so there was nothing to prevent the driver from being ejected and killed.
(Courtesy of San Diego Police Museum archives.)

World War II was especially difficult for SDPD officers and their cars. Because new cars weren't being made and even spare parts were tough to obtain, under no circumstances was an SDPD car to be driven more than 25 miles per shift. In this 1942 photo, Officer Tom Remington is seen at Ryan Field with an unknown military officer. (Courtesy of E.W. Kenney historic collection of the San Diego Police Museum.)

In the 1940s, the SDPD made a push to cut down on preventable traffic deaths by initiating a public awareness campaign of billboards and public service ads. The drive paid off and by the end of the decade traffic deaths were in a downward spiral. (Courtesy of E.W. Kenney collection of the San Diego Police Museum.)

The police ambulance was called to the scene after a Ryan test pilot crashed an experimental airplane at Lindbergh Field on January 21, 1947. The crash occurred when the plane's landing gear failed to deploy and the pilot was forced to do a belly landing. He survived. (Courtesy of E.W. Kenney historic collection of the San Diego Police Museum.)

Here is a glimpse inside the back of one of SDPD's first vehicles that was specifically equipped as an ambulance. Prior to this vehicle being purchased, it was not uncommon to transport injured parties and prisoners in the same vehicle—sometimes at the same time. (Courtesy of E.W. Kenney historic collection of the San Diego Police Museum.)

Who says policemen can't get into the holiday spirit? Officers Don Newby and Louie Howell used their police car as the centerpiece for their 1948 Christmas card. (Courtesy of Marsha Aleisi.)

Officer Frank Bonnet scratches his head when trying to figure out what the fine is for illegally parking a horse in this 1948 photograph. The buggy was part of a campaign gimmick by Don Smith, a candidate for U.S. Congress. (Courtesy of E.W. Kenney historic collection of the San Diego Police Museum.)

A squad of officers posed for this picture at police headquarters as they prepared to start their day doing school speed-zone enforcement. The battle to try and control pedestrian-versus-vehicle accidents was multifaceted. (Courtesy of E.W. Kenney historic collection of the San Diego Police Museum.)

It is possible that the SDPD operated the only police bowling alley in the world. Opened in 1947 in police headquarters, the four-lane alley was available to officers and their families at reduced rates. There was even a snack bar. Because of its lack of profitability, the alley was closed in 1952 and sold to an operation in Tempe, Arizona. (Courtesy of E.W. Kenney historic collection of the San Diego Police Museum.)

Chief Elmer Jansen looks on as one of his men checks a driver to determine whether or not he has had a little too much to drink. The roadblocks were a continuation of a "get tough on drunk drivers" campaign waged by the department. (Courtesy of Francis Jansen.)

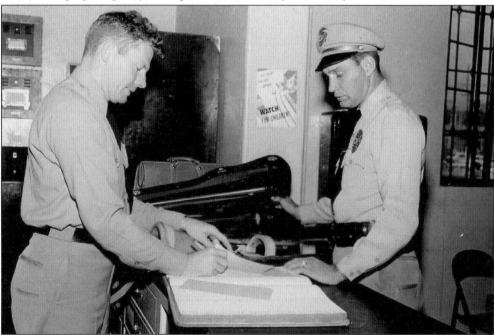

An officer checks a found violin into the police property room in this September 1952 photograph. Then, like now, if the owner cannot be located the instrument will wind up with other unclaimed property at the police auction. (Courtesy of E.W. Kenney historic collection of the San Diego Police Museum.)

Officers conduct an experiment using radar to catch speeders on Highway 395 in what is now Rancho Bernardo in this June 11, 1954 photograph. While officers commonly use radar today, this event was so significant that chief Jansen and a number of other city officials were on hand to watch. (Courtesy of E.W. Kenney historic collection of the San Diego Police Museum.)

Today, a modern radar unit can be held in an officer's hand and the speed display is digital. It wasn't always like that as this 1955 picture illustrates. (Courtesy of E.W. Kenney historic collection of the San Diego Police Museum.)

Before short sleeves became part of the uniform, on hot days officers were relieved to hear a code-9 that allowed them to remove their ties and roll the sleeves of their wool shirts up slightly. In this August 1955 photo, this officer's sleeves would be too high, however chief Jansen doesn't seem to mind as he wipes the sweat from his brow. (Courtesy of E.W. Kenney historic collection of the San Diego Police Museum.)

Sgt. Robert Crosby, Chief Elmer Jansen, and four policewomen wait for the television camera to roll as KFMB TV prepares a 1955 special on the return of policewomen within the SDPD after a 23-year absence. (Courtesy of E.W. Kenney historic collection of the San Diego Police Museum.)

Firemen look over the wreckage of what was once a San Diego police car in this March 11, 1957 photograph. Sgt. Harry Kay was driving the car and lost control while in a high-speed pursuit through Rose Canyon. He was killed instantly. Ironically, just hours before his death, Sergeant Kay was at the police academy teaching a class on safe vehicle operations. (Courtesy of E.W. Kenney historic collection.)

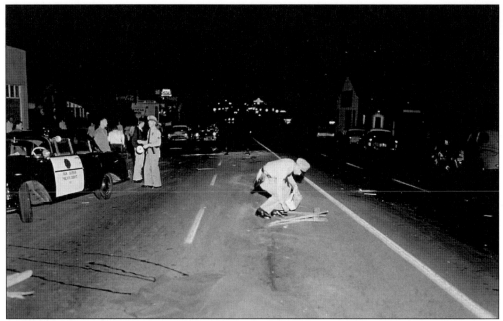

The body is still in the street as traffic officers investigate a fatal hit-and-run accident in this May 20, 1957 photograph. The suspect vehicle was recovered a short time after the collision and towed to police headquarters for further examination. (Courtesy of E.W. Kenney historic collection of the San Diego Police Museum.)

In a follow-up photograph, a traffic officer and detective take note of the large shattered imprint left on the windshield of the suspect car during an examination at police headquarters. The damage occurred when the victim went over the hood and his head struck the windshield. (Courtesy of E.W. Kenney historic collection of the San Diego Police Museum.)

Other than paperwork and waiting for the coroner and a tow truck, there's not much else that can be done at the scene of this November 4, 1957 car-versus-train crash at California Street and Laurel Street. (Courtesy of San Diego Police Museum archives.)

Seen here is Officer Rusty Giles on parking enforcement duty in May 1958. Shortly after the picture was taken, the responsibilities of maintaining orderly parking were transferred to civilian meter maids. (Courtesy of E.W. Kenney historic collection of the San Diego Police Museum.)

The cycles are brand new and their uniforms are crisp. An eager group of meter maids get one last inspection before heading out on patrol in this 1959 photo. In the 1970s, the group had their name changed to parking enforcement officers (PEOs). In a cost-cutting move in the early 1990s, the SDPD transferred all of its PEOs to the city's transportation department. (Courtesy of E.W. Kenney historic collection.)

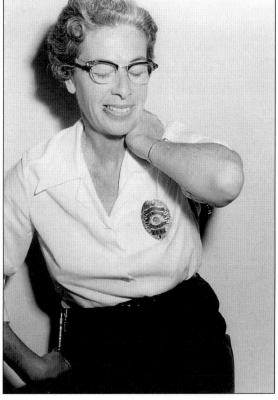

Police matron Bennett holds her neck in agony after being attacked by an inmate in the city jail in this August 1958 photograph. Matrons served the SDPD from 1912 until the 1960s. They worked in the jails handling female inmates and juveniles. (Courtesy of E.W. Kenney historic collection of the San Diego Police Museum.)

A traffic officer watches as a police recruit demonstrates what he has learned in the arrest-and-control portion of the 1959 police academy. (Courtesy of E.W. Kenney historic collection of the San Diego Police Museum.)

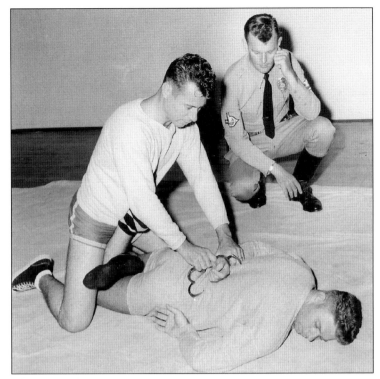

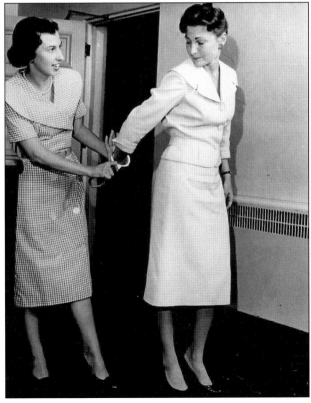

Just like their male counterparts, 1950s policewomen Pat McWilliams (left) and Sandra Kingston were expected to know when to arrest someone and how to properly use handcuffs. The first female detective on the SDPD certainly knew how to use them, for in 1913 she arrested two firemen for loitering and booked them into jail. Shortly thereafter, a very angry fire chief, Louis Almgren, showed up at the station demanding a face-to-face talk with her. (Courtesy of E.W. Kenney historic collection of the San Diego Police Museum.)

A crowd has gathered on El Cajon Boulevard just west of Florida Street hoping to catch a glimpse of a traffic accident directly across the street from a hospital. Unfortunately for the victim, this August 20, 1958 crash was fatal. (Courtesy of E.W. Kenney historic collection of the San Diego Police Museum.)

Chief Jansen addresses a police academy graduation in this late 1950s photograph. For many new officers they received their classroom training at the same time they gained on-the-job experience. Recruits attended class for a block of hours and then, on the same day, walked a beat for several more. Some new officers found themselves in situations where they didn't have class a certain day but they were given a beat assignment, or vice versa. The result was that many, if not all, worked seven days a week while in training. (Courtesy San Diego Police Museum archives.)

Even though this hall features knife-throwing games that would appeal to a rougher crowd, Detective Halley checks the pinball machines to make sure the games are not rigged or otherwise manipulated to make them unfair to the paying public. (Courtesy of E.W. Kenney historic collection of the San Diego Police Museum.)

An officer checks the gurney in his ambulance before heading out on patrol in this February 5, 1964 photograph. There were a number of officers assigned to ambulance duty alone, making it quite a feat to handle a trauma victim while driving to the hospital. The helmet the officer is wearing was standard issue for all uniformed patrolmen and sergeants from 1963 to 1973. (Courtesy of E.W. Kenney collection of the San Diego Police Museum.)

In the days before officers were assigned handheld radios, foot patrolmen relied upon call boxes to keep in touch with headquarters. A patrolman was expected to check in every 30 minutes. Some call boxes around the city were equipped with blue lights that would flash in the event an officer was needed prior to his check-in time. (Courtesy of E.W. Kenney collection of the San Diego Police Museum.)

Officer Bob Slaughter finds the water is just a little deeper than he thought when he pulled out of the front parking lot of police headquarters one rainy day in the 1960s. (Courtesy of San Diego Police Museum archives.)

Officer Terry Truitt trains officers on how to identify outlaw motorcycle gangs in this April 1966 photograph. During his time as an SDPD officer, Truitt developed an extensive knowledge of motorcycle gangs and was widely considered one of the foremost experts in the Western United States. (Courtesy of Terry Truitt.)

While scenes of police officers standing in the snow might be common in Detroit or Chicago, in San Diego they are very rare indeed. Officers Jerald Hill (left) and Howard Goldie had their snow photo taken in Rancho Bernardo in the late 1960s. (Courtesy of Det. Renee Hill.)

Chief Ray Hoobler (right) sits in the control room of KSON radio, where he just finished a stint as the station's "celebrity deejay for a day." During his September 1971 show, the chief talked about the problems faced by police and answered dozens of questions from citizens. To Hoobler's right is station president Dan McKinnon and deejay Gary Perkins. (Courtesy of Ray Hoobler.)

Most people wouldn't go into a dark alley for a million dollars. Cops do it everyday for a lot less. Officer Bob Szycmjac checks an alley in North Mission Beach on February 7, 1973. (Courtesy of Bob Lampert.)

An SDPD officer stands a post at the San Ysidro border checkpoint, waiting for cars heading south into Mexico. After passing this checkpoint, motorists would continue on to another one, this time operated by Mexican customs agents less than one mile down the road. Checkpoint duty was discontinued in the 1970s, when it was decided the federal government should handle it. (Courtesy of E.W. Kenney historic collection of the San Diego Police Museum.)

Officer Gene Rich is seen here with a cart of cigarettes, candy, and other items sold in the city jail. Just a few months after this October 1973 photo was taken, the city jail was closed and future arrestees were booked into a county facility. (Courtesy of E.W. Kenney historic collection of the San Diego Police Museum.)

Lt. James Harrell saved the day by taking a lost boy back to his family in Mission Beach. (Courtesy of Bob Lampert.)

From the late 1980s until the mid-1990s, professional photographer Sandra Small brought her 35-millimeter camera as she accompanied SDPD officers on a series of ride-alongs. Her close proximity to events as they unfolded resulted in an entire collection of historical images. (Courtesy of Sandra Small collection of the San Diego Police Museum.)

Officer Carolyn McDermod points to fresh graffiti she discovered while on patrol. Knowing how to read graffiti can often provide officers valuable information in their constant battle against street gangs. (Courtesy of Sandra Small collection of the San Diego Police Museum.)

With guns drawn and safety in numbers, officers are taking no chances with this high-risk vehicle stop that culminates in a successful arrest. (Courtesy of Sandra Small collection of the San Diego Police Museum.)

Detectives and scene specialists from the crime lab will come out to investigate crimes such as murder and serial rapes, but it is not uncommon to find specially trained patrol officers or agents doing the forensic work at non-life threatening shootings and stabbings. In this case, police agent Tony Pellegrino sets up evidence markers as the first step in his processing of the crime scene. (Courtesy of Sandra Small collection of the San Diego Police Museum.)

An undercover officer poses as a street prostitute along one of San Diego's most notorious strips. The man in the car, commonly known as a "john," had pulled over and solicited the officer for sex. She directed him to a nearby motel, where he was in for a surprise. (Courtesy of Sandra Small collection of the San Diego Police Museum.)

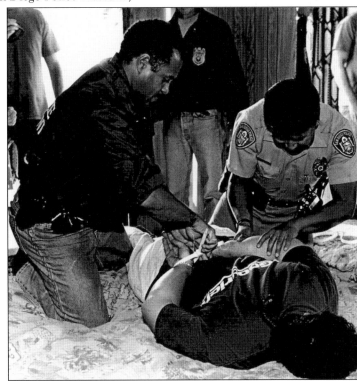

Officer Conrad DeCastro and NCIS special agent Karl Rodriguez spring into action seconds after the john walks through the door. Instead of finding an afternoon of pleasure, the john winds up with an arrest, an impounded car, and a pending court date. His troubles didn't stop there either. The car he was driving belonged to his boss. (Courtesy of Sandra Small collection of the San Diego Police Museum.)

79

Officers raided this drug house after neighbors complained about constant dealing. When they got inside they found the occupants living in filthy conditions without electricity or running water. (Courtesy of Sandra Small collection of the San Diego Police Museum.)

In the late 1980s, the city began to experience a violent crime rate not seen since the 1800s. In response, the SDPD created a team of specially trained and equipped uniformed officers for gang enforcement. Today the team is a permanent part of the Gang Investigations Unit. (Courtesy of Sandra Small collection of the San Diego Police Museum.)

Without barriers to use for cover should something go awry, officers are forced to make the best of it as they deal with a potentially dangerous situation at an East San Diego apartment complex. The incident ended peacefully. (Courtesy of Sandra Small collection of the San Diego Police Museum.)

Det. Steve McMillan discusses a crime scene with Officers Annie Anderson and Susan Righthouse. McMillan was investigating a robbery that just occurred at a commercial business. (Courtesy of Sandra Small collection of the San Diego Police Museum.)

As dramatic as this photo looks at first glance, a drive-by shooting about to occur, it is actually staged. The photo was part of an educational series done in the early 1990s by SDPD officers to illustrate the stark realities of gang life. For a variety of reasons, the project was never used. (Courtesy of Sandra Small collection of the San Diego Police Museum.)

Mayor Maureen O'Connor and councilman John Hartley accompany City Heights residents as they march in a neighborhood watch rally to take back the streets in the early 1990s. The SDPD was a pioneering agency in Neighborhood Watch, with citizens and police partnering to reduce crime. In neighborhoods where it is used, the effect on the crime rate can be dramatic. (Courtesy of Sandra Small collection of the San Diego Police Museum.)

Even with the push to institute neighborhood watch, not all residents of City Heights were ready to sign up. (Courtesy of Sandra Small collection of the San Diego Police Museum.)

Officers use the utmost caution in exercising a high-risk vehicle stop. After clearing suspects from the passenger section of a car, the trunk must be checked. With guns drawn, officers are ready for any surprises. (Courtesy of Sandra Small collection of the San Diego Police Museum.)

Officers David Jennings and Annie Anderson are caught off guard when a routine contact gets emotional. A young boy has suddenly realized that his loved one is going to jail. (Courtesy of Sandra Small collection of the San Diego Police Museum.)

While television portrays police work as non-stop action, high-speed chases and shootouts, in reality paperwork is what occupies much of a patrol officer's time. In this case, officers use a police storefront to complete their reports. (Courtesy of Sandra Small collection of the San Diego Police Museum.)

A valuable tool modern police officers has is the helicopter. Named ABLE (Air Borne Law Enforcement), the aircraft is manned by a pilot and observer and is available to respond to almost any emergency. The helicopter provides officers on the ground with an extra set of eyes and can be invaluable in high-speed chases and searches. (Courtesy of Sandra Small collection of the San Diego Police Museum.)

Even though uniformed female patrol officers have served the SDPD since the early 1970s, many citizens were still caught off guard when motorcycle officer Lori Bach stopped them. Bach, who had joined the motor squad in the early 1990s, recalled it was not uncommon to get to the window of the offending motorists car only to be addressed as "sir." (Courtesy of Sgt. Lori Bach.)

Tattoos can play a part in identification. Before they became a fashion trend, many criminals were getting them. The markings can tell officers of an arrestee's associates, gang affiliation, and even when and where they served time in prison. (Courtesy of Sandra Small collection of the San Diego Police Museum.)

Officer Bill Albrektsen makes an arrest in an East San Diego alley in the early 1990s. Despite being one of the smallest per capita police departments in the country, the SDPD annually boasts some of the highest arrest numbers. Perhaps in a direct correlation, San Diego enjoys one of the lowest crimes rates of any big city. (Courtesy of Sandra Small collection.)

Officer Troy Gibson embarks on a citizen's least favorite interaction with a police officer—the issuance of a traffic citation. Contrary to popular folklore, the California Vehicle Code prohibits police agencies from having a ticket quota and officers do not work for commission. (Courtesy of Sandra Small collection of the San Diego Police Museum.)

Officers Kim Robinson and Brett Burkett signal that their gas masks are working as they undergo tear-gas training at the police academy. Many officers describe the gas chamber experience as one of the worst things they have ever had to deal with. (Courtesy of San Diego Police Museum.)

After the 1999 World Trade Organization riots in Seattle caused hundreds of thousands of dollars in damage, the SDPD wanted to be ready for the Biotech 2001 convention. Many of the groups that caused trouble in Seattle made it known they were headed to San Diego. The department's response was to put a high-visibility presence on the streets and to enforce all laws. In case rioting broke out, officers were ready to respond quickly to break it up. (Courtesy San Diego Police Museum archive.)

Six
INVESTIGATIONS

For reports taken and arrests made, a detective must make an investigative follow-up to ensure justice is done. The detective then forwards the results to a prosecutor and the courts for adjudication. The first detective on the SDPD was Harry Von Den Berg, who assumed the position in 1907. He investigated everything from theft to murder. In 1913, a female detective, E. Belle Robinson, was hired to investigate crimes against children. In 1927, detectives began to be assigned to specialized units such as robbery and homicide. Today, there are more than 300 detectives in the SDPD, and they investigate a wide array of crimes both reactively and proactively.

Det. P. Harry Von Den Berg is shown here (stocky man in center of picture) outside of police headquarters at 1026 Second Avenue, c. 1908. The men had just came back from a raid and are standing in front of stolen horses and buggies that were recovered. (Courtesy of E.W. Kenney historic collection of the San Diego Police Museum.)

Det. Sgt. George Churchman examines the vehicle that killed motorcycle officer Robert Powers on July 17, 1928. Powers was riding his motorcycle at 10:30 p.m. on Barnett Avenue just north of Ryan Field when he was struck head-on by a drunk driver who was on the wrong side of the road without headlights. Powers was thrown through the windshield and died before ambulances could arrive. (Courtesy of E.W. Kenney historic collection of the San Diego Police Museum.)

The SDPD crime lab had been in existence for almost a full decade when this late 1940s photograph was taken. It was state of the art for its time. Today, the SDPD crime lab is recognized across the country as an innovator in forensic science. (Courtesy of E.W. Kenney historic collection of the San Diego Police Museum.)

Officers and detectives look into the brush where maintenance workers discovered human bones in September 1948. A follow-up investigation revealed the remains belonged to a woman missing since December 1940. Evidence at the scene led to the cause of death being ruled a suicide. (Courtesy of E.W. Kenney historic collection of the San Diego Police Museum.)

Officers try to determine if a body found along the road near Mission Bay is the result of a traffic accident, natural causes, or something more sinister such as murder. A closer examination showed multiple injuries on the victim, and homicide detectives were called. (Courtesy San Diego Police Museum archives.)

Lt. Walter Scott examines a .22 caliber revolver that was used in a February 1951 murder. The weapon was fired 16 times, but on the next-to-last shot a bullet became lodged in the barrel. The next shot caused a portion of the barrel to explode. (Courtesy of E.W. Kenney historic collection of the San Diego Police Museum.)

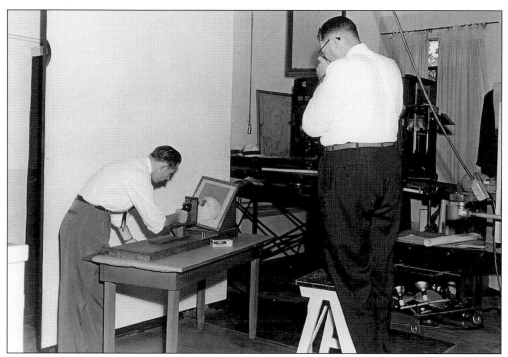

Detectives use forensic tests, in this case shooting a rubber mask, to reconstruct a suspicious shooting in 1955. The detectives are measuring powder burns to determine if the victim committed suicide or was murdered. (Courtesy of San Diego Police Museum archives.)

Members of the press join curious neighbors behind the crime-scene rope as officers investigate a 1956 shooting on Forty-fifth Street in southeastern San Diego. The victim ultimately died of his wounds. (Courtesy San Diego Police Museum archives.)

In this 1958 photograph, officers and a detective discuss the evidence from a shootout that occurred in a southeastern San Diego liquor store. The trouble started when an off-duty officer walked into the store as it was being robbed. The officer traded rounds with the suspect who was ultimately killed. The officer was sent to the hospital, but fortunately he eventually recovered. (Courtesy of E.W. Kenney historic collection of the San Diego Police Museum.)

Officer Robert Filley dusts for fingerprints at the scene of a robbery of an adult bookstore knowing a positive match will be 100-percent proof that the suspect was at the scene. It will then be up to detectives to prove the suspect actually committed the crime. (Courtesy of Sandra Small collection of the San Diego Police Museum.)

Seven

UNIFORMS, INSIGNIA, AND CARS

The 1885 city marshals were the first San Diego lawmen to wear uniforms. The men wore dark blue dusters with silver badges reading "San Diego Police." When the SDPD was formed in 1889, they adopted a similar uniform but with a shorter coat. The men were required to wear it whenever they were in public, on or off duty. In 1915, the department converted from blue to green, but went back to blue for the 1935 exposition. In 1947, the SDPD adopted a tan uniform. Agency patches were added in 1989, and in 1996 the department converted back to the traditional blue.

Officer Pat Oviatt (left) and a fireman enjoy some fresh air on a downtown sidewalk around 1913. Prior to 1935, patrol officers such as Oviatt were not allowed to display their weapons outside of their coats. The result is that many people who view old-time photographs assume the officers are unarmed. (Courtesy of E.W. Kenney historic collection of the San Diego Police Museum.)

FOR EXCEEDING THE
SPEED LIMIT

Officer Paul Plaistead (left) and his partner take a moment from their walking beat to mug for the camera with what was later labeled a speeding donkey. In reality the animal was holding up traffic as he and his owner slowly pulled a cart through city streets as cars backed up behind them. The pearl-gray helmets the men are wearing were only worn during the summer. (Courtesy of E.W. Kenney historic collection of the San Diego Police Museum.)

A motorcycle officer models the high-collar, olive drab uniform worn by SDPD from 1915–1935. The uniform was made of heavy wool and was about as comfortable as an Army blanket. It was also the only authorized uniform regardless of the weather. (Courtesy of E.W. Kenney historic collection of the San Diego Police Museum.)

This is an excellent look at a 1930s mounted officer with the now very rare horseman's patch just under his left shoulder. From 1913 until around 1940, mounted officers wore a patch showing a horse head in the center of a wagon wheel. The four hash marks on the officer's forearm represent five years of service per stripe. (Courtesy of E.W. Kenney historic collection of the San Diego Police Museum.)

It was rare to see an officer standing next to the chief of police without a hat. In this 1937 photograph, Chief George Sears and a sergeant stop to mug for the camera at the Organ Pavilion in Balboa Park. The pins on their collars are the centerpieces of their shield, a City of San Diego seal with "police" under it. All officers above the rank of sergeant wore the pins. (Courtesy of E.W. Kenney historic collection of the San Diego Police Museum.)

Sgt. Wayne Gray models the 1940 SDPD uniform without the dress coat. The gold band around his hat was authorized only for sergeants and above. In 1947, all officers were allowed to wear the gold band with their hat. Today, the old rule is the modern way. Only supervisors can have a gold band. (Courtesy of E.W. Kenney historic collection of the San Diego Police Museum.)

An officer and a sergeant leave headquarters to head out on patrol in the early 1940s. Despite its classic lines and fancy paint job, the car did not have air conditioning, heat, power steering, power brakes, or even seat belts. It is quite primitive when compared to the cars modern officers drive. (Courtesy of E.W. Kenney collection of the San Diego Police Museum.)

A.P.B. CAR

Note "Clock", Flares, Fire Extinguisher, Siren works from horn ring.

The inside of a 1940s patrol car was a lot simpler then than it is now. Take a passenger car, add a two-way radio, a spotlight, and a pacing clock, and the car is transformed. Today, completely outfitting a police car can take several weeks. (Courtesy of San Diego Police Museum archives.)

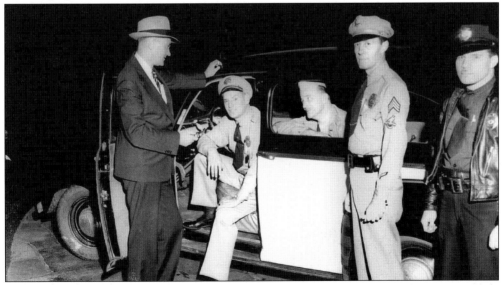

In 1940, the SDPD was broken up into three sections: patrol, traffic, and detectives. While detectives wore plain clothes (always with a hat), one might expect that traffic and patrol would wear the same colored uniform, but they didn't. In 1940, traffic officers choose to wear an all-tan uniform while patrol continued to wear the blue (adopted in 1935). The division ended in 1947, when Chief Jansen ordered the entire department into tan. (Courtesy of E.W. Kenney historic collection of the San Diego Police Museum.)

The January 1944 photograph of Sgt. Frank Logan and his squad is one of the last ever taken where officers were required to wear the "over the shoulder" Sam Brown gun belt as part of their regular uniform. Within days of the shoot, officers were ordered to remove the strap as it was becoming a safety hazard. (Courtesy of E.W. Kenney historic collection of the San Diego Police Museum.)

As World War II raged overseas and one-third of the SDPD had been drafted, local men pitched in to help back home as volunteer members of the police auxiliary. Without their help it is likely the SDPD would not have been able to function. When the war ended in 1945, the auxiliary was disbanded. However, just five years later it was clear they were missed, so the police reserve officer program was established. (Courtesy of E.W. Kenney historic collection of the San Diego Police Museum.)

Brand-new badges await 22 new officers in this early 1950s photo. For badge collectors, a gold-filled, three-digit San Diego police patrolman badge commands some of the highest prices on the collectors market. For the men who are about to be issued the badge, it is valuable as well. It represents a lot of hard work and sacrifice. (Courtesy of E.W. Kenney historic collection of the San Diego Police Museum.)

Officers Bert Wright and Robert Schroers take a moment to show off their new 1954 Jeep four-by-four they will be using to patrol beaches. The photograph was taken on the patio of police headquarters on 801 West Market Street. (Courtesy of E.W. Kenney historic collection of the San Diego Police Museum.)

The patio of police headquarters is as good a place as any for a dress uniform inspection, as seen in this 1950s photograph. The jacket the officers are wearing was commonly referred to as the Eisenhower and was designed by SDPD. Within a few years of its adoption, most other San Diego County agencies were also wearing the coat as part of their dress uniform. (Courtesy of E.W. Kenney historic collection of the San Diego Police Museum.)

Officers prepare to load the trunk of a three-wheeled motorcycle in this May 1955 photograph. While most cycles were used for parking enforcement, this one was used for traffic-accident investigations. (Courtesy of E.W. Kenney historic collection of the San Diego Police Museum.)

A communications and electrical engineer installs a new police radio and antenna in a patrol car. Note how much space the 1950s tube and transistor system occupies in the trunk. (Courtesy of E.W. Kenney historic collection of the San Diego Police Museum.)

The long blue coat and Sam Brown gun belt, both holdovers from the 1940s, were brought back for the 1957 funeral of Sgt. Harry Kay. When the SDPD converted to tan uniforms in 1947, officers were still allowed to wear the blue coat for formal occasions. By the mid 1950s, it was replaced by the Eisenhower jacket. It appears that this is the last time this uniform combination was ever worn. (Courtesy of E.W. Kenney historic collection of the San Diego Police Museum.)

Technically speaking, this officer would be out of uniform, however, it appears he could be doing it for a good cause . . . well, sort of. Note the camera in one hand and the scrub brush in the other. The officer is apparently ribbing an off-camera fireman who is trying to clean up a mess from a fire. (Courtesy of San Diego Police Museum archives.)

This 1960 photograph of Officer Kilgore using the radio provides an excellent look inside a police car of the era. Clearly the car was not built for comfort or aesthetics. (Courtesy of E.W. Kenney historic collection of the San Diego Police Museum.)

A 1962 Plymouth parked on the patio of the old police headquarters provides an excellent look at the simplicity of some of the older SDPD cars. (Courtesy of San Diego Police Museum archives.)

An officer rounding the tree at a disturbance call gets his man red-handed. Or is it red-coated? This lighthearted 1963 photo was used on the cover of the *Fall In* magazine, a monthly in-house publication. (Courtesy of San Diego Police Museum archives.)

Motorcycle officer Don Kepner models the just-approved short-sleeve uniform for SDPD secretary Janet Kunicki. Chief Wes Sharp approved the shirts in July 1965. It was an instant morale boost to many officers who had suffered through hot summers wearing long-sleeve wool shirts and neckties. (Courtesy of E.W. Kenney historic collection of the San Diego Police Museum.)

Officer Bill Shewbert would get a two-day suspension for not having his helmet on, but this photo gives a great look at the simplicity of the uniform of the era. The white cars were introduced in the late 1960s to usher in a less aggressive image. By the late 1980s, they were a thing of the past as black and whites made a comeback. (Courtesy of E.W. Kenney historic collection of the San Diego Police Museum.)

Off-road enforcement is why this officer is wearing a cotton jumpsuit with drawstring legs and tucked-in boots. While this is only one officer, off-road enforcement became a full-time job for an entire team in the 1980s. Called the "Tac-team," they were not only responsible for off-road enforcement but they were also used at the border, the beach, and at special events. (Courtesy of E.W. Kenney historic collection of the San Diego Police Museum.)

In 1988, the SDPD introduced a shoulder patch for uniformed officers. After almost 100 years without an agency patch, it was decided a change was needed; yet the reaction was mixed. Some officers loved them, while others saw no need for them. When the department returned to blue uniforms in 1996, the patches were changed from brown to blue and gold. (Courtesy San Diego Police Museum archives.)

In 1989, to recognize the 100-year anniversary of the SDPD, the department allowed officers to wear a commemorative badge. It was a composite of the first two SDPD badges, and the rank rocker added above was not something any SDPD badge ever had. Nonetheless, it was exceptionally popular. The badge was officially retired January 1, 1990. (Badge courtesy of Sgt. Bob Dare.)

Sgt. Tony Johnson (center) and reserve sergeant Rocky Ventittelli discover some of the benefits of working on the beach enforcement team. Not only do they not have to shine their cloth badges, no one can keep their hands off the uniform. (Courtesy San Diego Police Museum archives.)

Police communications have made serious advances since the dispatch system was first introduced in 1932. As this 1996 photograph illustrates, the communications center has moved from tubes and transistors towards a more computerized process. (Courtesy of San Diego Police Museum archives.)

Unless you consider the Green Bay Police Department, it's unlikely this hat would be seen as official uniform headwear anywhere. With San Diego hosting the Superbowl, Officers Greg Lindstrom and Louie Valenzuela get into the sprit of the game in this 1998 photograph. Even with the support of the two officers, the Denver Broncos beat the Packers 31-24. (Courtesy of Sandra Small collection of the San Diego Police Museum.)

As many places around the country are beginning to see a change in seasons and a drop in temperature, an SDPD officer still gets to enjoy summer in October as he rides his patrol ATV in the surf. (Courtesy of Sandra Small collection of the San Diego Police Museum.)

Eight

HUB LOAN

The Hub Loan shootout of April 8, 1965, began when a man walked into the Hub Loan Pawn Shop at Fifth and F Streets and murdered the storeowner. Officers converged before the killer had a chance to escape and the gunfight was on. The incident became so out of control that off-duty officers who saw the battle on television drove down, emptied their guns into the building, and left. The incident ended when Sgt. Allen Brown went into the store and shot the suspect. The gunman survived and was sentenced to death. When he heard his fate he proclaimed, "If I had known I was going to get death, I would have killed more people." A 1972 ban on capital punishment overturned the killer's sentence and today he is a free man.

Officers use a beverage truck as cover outside the Hub Loan Company as they discuss strategies to end the shootout. An armored car, brought in as a shield from gunfire, can also be seen outside the building. (Courtesy of Allen Brown.)

Bullets are striking the other side of the vehicle as Officers Bob Augustine and Bob Wierma use the armored car for cover while they catch their breath and reload their weapons. (Courtesy of Allen Brown.)

Sgt. Allen Brown directs officers into position from behind the beverage truck. Seconds later, he would climb onto it to take a shot at the suspect. (Courtesy of Allen Brown.)

Officers scramble for cover and better positions as bullets fly through the air during the Hub Loan shootout. Note the officer on the far left with explosives in his right hand; to his left are three reporters kneeling down. (Courtesy of Allen Brown.)

Shotgun shells litter the street as officers fire into the Hub Loan Pawn Shop. The boots on the left belong to US Navy Shore patrolman Frank Morales, who volunteered to come to the scene with concussion grenades. Before throwing the grenades, officers wanted to try and use tear gas. It would prove to be a mistake. (Courtesy of Allen Brown.)

Reporters and officers run for cover after the wind blew the tear gas back into the street. Minutes later Morales threw in the grenades, blowing out all of the first-floor windows in the building. (Courtesy of Allen Brown.)

Sergeant Brown pauses to reload as shots ring out in all directions. Since the tear gas and grenades had no effect, officers knew the only way to end the shootout was to go in and get the suspect. While it is a little hard to discern in this photograph, Brown has a large piece of metal strapped to the front of his chest to act as a bulletproof shield. It proved to be too heavy and impractical, and within minutes Brown discarded it. (Courtesy of Allen Brown.)

With bullets whizzing by his head, Allen Brown crawls to the door of the Hub Loan Pawn Shop. Brown is not only trying to locate the shooter, he is also trying to see if the storeowner, 61-year-old Louis Richards who is lying in the doorway, is still alive. Brown was able to reach into the store and drag Richards out, but it was too late. Minutes later, Brown shot the suspect and the four-hour gunfight was over. (Courtesy of Allen Brown.)

An officer armed with a Thompson submachine gun debriefs a fellow officer after the shootout. Officer Sam Chasteen originally fired the machine gun into the building, but had to be evacuated after he injured his head ducking from a bullet. (Courtesy of Allen Brown.)

The shootout is barely over and already reporters want to talk to Allen Brown. It was then they discovered that while Brown was in the building the gunman snuck up behind him and began pulling the trigger of a handgun. Fortunately for Brown the gun was loaded with the wrong ammunition so it didn't fire. (Courtesy of Allen Brown.)

After the shootout, officers were astonished to find out exactly how many weapons the gunman had access to. Clearly the shootout could have lasted many hours longer. (Courtesy of Allen Brown.)

In the aftermath of the shootout, there are reports to be filed. A detective counts up just a few of the more than 800 bullet holes that were left behind. Today, the Hub Loan Pawn Shop is a popular coffee shop and most of its patrons have no idea what once occurred there. However, if you know where to look, one can still find a few bullet holes on the outside of the building. (Courtesy of Allen Brown.)

Sgt. Allen Brown and a deputy district attorney review a scale model of the Hub Loan building as the state prepares a case against the gunman. (Courtesy of Allen Brown.)

The aftermath of the Hub Loan shootout demonstrated why a special tactics team was needed for large scale, violent incidents. In response, the department quickly formed the Anti-Sniper Platoon (ASP). Allen Brown was promoted to lieutenant and was told to pick officers to serve under him. In this 1967 photo, taken at USMC base Camp Pendleton, Brown demonstrates sniper techniques to some of the new officers. Many years after the formation of ASP, the name was changed to SWAT. (Courtesy of Allen Brown.)

Nine

THE MOTORCYCLE SQUAD

The original name of the motor squad carried the bravado title of "The Flying Squad." At the time, with road conditions and the equipment the men used, the name was fitting. Most San Diego streets were unpaved and leather gloves were the only protection for early motor officers. The first motorcycle officers had to purchase their own machines, but they were paid an extra $25 per month. Today, the motor squad has access to the best equipment and safety gear available, but it is still dangerous duty.

SDPD's first motorcycle officer was Herbert Hill. Seen here with his ride shortly after his 1911 appointment, Hill was primarily tasked with enforcing speed laws and accident investigation. Newspaper accounts of the era reported Mrs. Hill also liked to ride the motorcycle, and the two would often take turns taking a spin in the country. (Courtesy of E.W. Kenney historic collection of the San Diego Police Museum.)

Not too long after Hill began the motor squad, Officer Leonard Freshour was assigned to join him. By the late 1930s, the squad totaled more than 50 officers. (Courtesy of E.W. Kenney historic collection of the San Diego Police Museum.)

Chief James Patrick took a few minutes of his time to jump into a sidecar to have his photo taken with several motor officers and civilian cycle enthusiasts. As one can see upon closer examination of the 1923 photograph, there weren't the same uniformity standards for attire as seen with today's modern officer. (Courtesy of E.W. Kenney historic collection of the San Diego Police Museum.)

Officer Clarence Renner was one of many hired between the 1920s and the 1950s specifically as a motorcycle officer. Prior to that, and under today's rules, an officer must serve as a patrol officer before he or she can be considered for motorcycle duty. (Courtesy of E.W. Kenney historic collection of the San Diego Police Museum.)

Apparently, Officer Renner wasn't the only one in his family who enjoyed motorcycles. Rosie Renner snapped this photo as she walked her husband outside to see him off to work. It was then they discovered the family cat had other ideas about who owned the motorcycle. (Courtesy of E.W. Kenney historic collection of the San Diego Police Museum.)

It's not uncommon for motorcycle officers to lead parades, but in this instance the line of cars aren't celebrating anything civic; they are real estate buyers eager to get in on the opening of San Diego's newest subdivision, Morrison's Marscene Park. In this 1927 photograph, the gates have just opened and the buyers are pouring in. While the name of Morrison's Marscene Park still exists, few San Diegans have ever heard of the area. It is located at Forty-third and Market Streets. (Courtesy of E.W. Kenney historic collection of the San Diego Police Museum.)

Officer Frank Bonnet goes over a few last-minute details before the dressed-up car takes to the streets to advertise and sell tickets to the Speed Cops Ball. The ball was an annual event and the proceeds benefited motorcycle officers who were injured in the line of duty. (Courtesy of E.W. Kenney historic collection of the San Diego Police Museum.)

Chief George Sears and the entire motorcycle squad posed in front of the county administration/city hall building in this November 11, 1938 photograph. Depending on your perspective, the squad was either large then, or is very small now. Despite the population of the city of San Diego increasing five-fold since 1938, the motorcycle squad has stayed exactly the same size. (Courtesy of E.W. Kenney historic collection of the San Diego Police Museum.)

The push to sell tickets to the Speed Cops Ball was everywhere—even secretaries couldn't escape it. Actually, this 1944 photo was taken to promote the ball, and the ladies were under no obligation to purchase. (Courtesy of E.W. Kenney historic collection of the San Diego Police Museum.)

Sgt. Walt Hunting models the full-dress uniform for motorcycle officers in the 1940s. On his right shoulder is the rare traffic division patch that was worn only on the dress coat, and only for a few years. (Courtesy of E.W. Kenney historic collection of the San Diego Police Museum.)

Traffic tickets and accident investigation aren't the only task of motorcycle officers; they are also the uniformed presence for dignitary protection. In this case, it was a 1970s visit to San Diego by Pres. Jimmy Carter. (Courtesy of San Diego Police Museum.)

Sgt. Pat McLarney stops to have his photo taken on the last day of the tan uniforms. After 48 years, on the next day the morning shift reported in their blues. (Courtesy of San Diego Police Museum.)

The National Transportation Safety Board used to advertise that "You can learn a lot from a dummy. Buckle your seatbelt." Another good lesson is never to ride double on a motorcycle built for one. The crash test dummies were on hand for a traffic education seminar, and used an SDPD bike for this humorous photo. (Courtesy of San Diego Police Museum.)

Police work can be rewarding, yet it can also be dangerous. In the 1980s, the SDPD had the highest per capita officer mortality rate in the United States. Through aggressive retraining, by the year 2000 it was the lowest. The honor guard salutes the memorial outside of headquarters that pays respect to all known SDPD officers who have made the supreme sacrifice. (Courtesy of San Diego Police Museum archives.)

San Diego City Marshals

* Sidney Livingston	February 1850–May 1850
Agoston Haraszathy	*May 1850–December 31, 1851*
** George Hooper	January 1852–February 1852
City Marshals office disbanded	*February 1852–1862*
** James McCoy	1862–February 1869
Alexander Young	*February 1869–September 1869*
Philip Crosthwaite	September 1869–August 1872
Adolph Gassen	*August 1872–May 26, 1874*
A.F. Knowles	May 26, 1874–May 1876
Albert Stowe	*May 1876–July 1876*
Thomas M. Turner	July 1876–July 1, 1878
James Russell (acting)	*July 1, 1878–February 1, 1879*
City Marshals office disbanded	February 6, 1879–June 1885
Joseph Coyne	*June 1885–May 31, 1889*
City Marshals office disbanded	May 31, 1889

* Was appointed prior to San Diego being officially incorporated as a U.S. city. ** Also served a concurrent term as county sheriff

Chiefs of the San Diego Police Department

Joseph Coyne	*May 14, 1889–May 26, 1891*
William Crawford	May 27, 1891–July 27, 1891
William H. Pringle	*July 28, 1891–August 27, 1891*
Jacob Brenning	August 28, 1891–May 9, 1897
James Russell	*May 10, 1897–May 4, 1899*
Edward "Ned" Bushyhead	May 5, 1899–May 31, 1903
Albert Thomas	*June 1, 1903–June 16, 1907*
George W. Moulton	June 17, 1907–September 3, 1907
William T. Neely	*September 4, 1907–April 30, 1909*
Jefferson "Keno" Wilson	May 3, 1909–January 10, 1917
Joseph Steer	*January 11, 1917–May 4, 1917*
James A. Patrick (acting)	May 5, 1917–October 9, 1917
Steward P. McMullen	*October 10, 1917–April 8, 1919*
James A. Patrick	April 9, 1919–May 31, 1927
Joseph V. Doran	*June 1, 1927–May 12, 1929*
Arthur R. Hill	May 13, 1929–May 3, 1931
Percival J. Benbough	*May 4, 1931–August 3, 1931*
Harry Scott	August 26, 1931–June 11, 1932
John T. Peterson	*June 12, 1932–July 31, 1932*
Robert P. Newsom	August 1, 1932–June 4, 1933
Harry Raymond	*June 5, 1933–September 1, 1933*
John T. Peterson	September 2, 1933–September 6, 1934
George M. Sears	*September 7, 1934–April 27, 1939*
Harry J. Kelly (acting)	April 28, 1939–July 18, 1939
John T. Peterson	*July 19, 1939–March 20, 1940*
Clifford Peterson	March 21, 1940–October 15, 1947
Adam E. "Elmer" Jansen	*October 16, 1947–January 7, 1962*
Wesley S. Sharp	January 8, 1962–January 3, 1968
Olif James "O.J." Roed	*January 4, 1968–March 11, 1971*
Raymond L. Hoobler	March 11, 1971–September 9, 1975
William B. Kolender	*September 10, 1975–July 29, 1988*
Robert W. Burgreen	July 30, 1988–May 17, 1993
Gerald Sanders	*May 17, 1993–May 16, 1999*
Keith W. Enerson (acting)	May 17, 1999–May 26, 1999

Raul David Bejarano | May 26, 1999–May 25, 2003
John Welter (acting) | May 26, 2003–August 4, 2003
William Lansdowne | August 4, 2003–Present

CHIEFS OF THE EAST SAN DIEGO POLICE DEPARTMENT

C.W. Justice	November 1912–Unknown
Frank Hyatt	Unknown–1914
Jason Ayers	1914–1918
Bill Gray	1918–1922
Nathaniel "Nat" McHorney Jr.	1922–December 31, 1923

SAN DIEGO CITY LAW ENFORCEMENT MORTALITY ROSTER

* Deputy city marshal Richard Freeman	November 1851
* Deputy city marshal Thomas B. O'Rourke	September 8, 1888
Motorcycle officer Emery E. Campbell	August 27, 1913
* Patrolman John V. McCann	December 7, 1913
Motorcycle sergeant Oliver S. Hopkins	July 2, 1915
Patrolman Walter B. Holcomb	October 21, 1918
Motorcycle officer Joseph S. Lee	March 19, 1921
Det. Charles R. Harris	April 2, 1927
Motorcycle officer Robert L. Powers	June 16, 1928
* Patrolman Lewis A. Lusk	September 30, 1928
Patrolman Robert B. McPherson	September 19, 1929
Motorcycle officer Edward J. Moore Jr.	January 15, 1933
* Capt. Robert P. Newsom	February 11, 1936
Sgt. Thomas A. Keays	October 20, 1937
* Motorcycle officer Frank S. Connors	January 9, 1938
Motorcycle officer Henry J. Goodrich	September 7, 1940
* Patrolman Frank B. Myrick	June 17, 1944
Patrolman Robert F. Bowers	December 12, 1955
Sgt. Harry Kay Jr.	March 11, 1957
Patrolman Michael J. Bushman	November 25, 1963
Sgt. Robert J. Everitt	December 7, 1964
* Cadet Allen D. Mortensen	March 23, 1969
Patrolman James P. Lewis	December 29, 1970
Sgt. Fred J. Edwards	October 7, 1971
Officer Denis W. Allen	April 1, 1977
Officer Archie C. Buggs	October 4, 1978
Officer Michael T. Anaya	March 21, 1979
Officer Dennis G. Gonzales	June 25, 1979
Officer Harry K. Tiffany	June 6, 1981
Officer Ronald R. Ebeltoff	June 6, 1981
Officer Kirk L. Johnson	February 22, 1983
* Officer James J. Carney Jr.	March 13, 1983
Officer Kimberly S. Tonahill	September 14, 1984
Officer Timothy J. Ruopp	September 14, 1984
Agent Thomas E. Riggs	March 31, 1985
Officer Jerry L. Hartless	January 9, 1988
Officer Ronald W. Davis	September 17, 1991
* Officer Donna P. Mauzy	June 23, 2001
Officer Gerald K. Griffin Jr.	April 25, 2003
Officer Terry W. Bennett	June 26, 2003

* Not on official SDPD roster for a variety of reasons, however, all either died on duty as a city marshal or in service to their country after being drafted from the ranks, or they perished in duty-related circumstances.